THE RAILWAYS OF ABERDEEN

150 Years of History

Dr. John A.N. Emslie (1936 - 2000)
This book is dedicated to the memory of John Emslie,
Honorary President of the Great North of Scotland Railway Association,
whose enthusiasm for and knowledge of Scotland's railways
has been an inspiration to many.

ISBN 0 902343 10 6

The Railways *of* Aberdeen

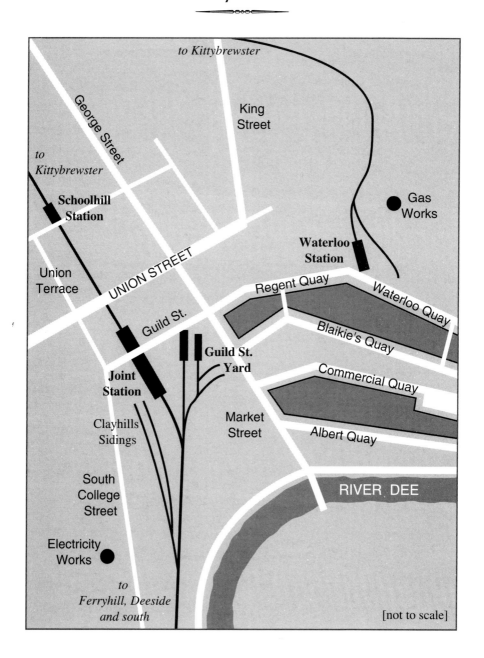

[not to scale]

Foreword

150 years ago, on March 16th 1850, a steam locomotive crossed the new River Dee Viaduct for the first time into Aberdeen's original railway station at Ferryhill. This momentous event in Aberdeen's history, reputedly watched by thousands who had gathered at the mere rumour that it was to make an appearance, led to an era when Aberdonians, for the first time, could partake of convenient, quick and relatively inexpensive travel.

Today, in the year 2000, despite the dominance of road and air transport, railways are still important to Aberdeen in the movement of passengers and goods.

This book is the Great North of Scotland Railway Association's contribution to the celebration of the 150th anniversary of the coming of the railways to Aberdeen, and provides a photographic history of developments over the years. Some of the illustrations may be familiar to readers, others have never been published before. The following pages will however prove of interest both to the local historian and to the railway enthusiast.

Keith G. Jones,
March, 2000.

LNER Class D41, number 6908, and D40, number 6848, make a fine sight as they prepare to depart on a northbound express, about 1930.

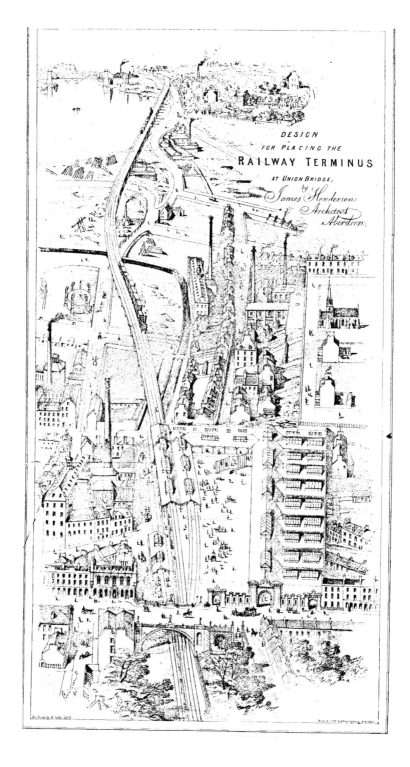

Proposed railway terminus at Market Street, Aberdeen, dating from the 1840s, prior to the plan being dropped in favour of the Guild Street site. The archway appears to be a smaller version of the Brandenburg Gate in Berlin! (Aberdeen City Council — Arts and Recreation Dept.)

Introduction

FOR centuries Aberdeen relied on the sea for transport, with trading connections to Northern Europe, particularly Holland, the Baltic States and the Hanseatic Ports. Other vessels plied the stormy East Coast of Britain from Shetland and Orkney to Leith, Tyneside, the Humber and the Thames. The road network remained generally poor until around the end of the eighteenth century. With the coming of the turnpike roads, travel throughout the North of Scotland became easier, and by the 1830s, a network of stage and mail coaches radiated from Aberdeen. An additional incentive to trade was the opening of the Aberdeenshire Canal from Waterloo Quay, Aberdeen, in 1805. A passenger boat provided a public service from Kittybrewster to Port Elphinstone, just south of Inverurie.

Aberdeen had featured in railway proposals as early as 1827, when Robert Stephenson had projected a line from the south, through the Vale of Strathmore, to the city. In the following decade, various further schemes were discussed, but it was 1845 before the Aberdeen Railway Company obtained powers to construct a railway from Aberdeen to Friockheim and Guthrie, near Forfar. This provided the final link in a network of railways which connected the city with Edinburgh, Glasgow, Carlisle and London.

Facing page: This plan, dated 1850, shows a proposed station at Union Bridge designed by a prominent Aberdeen architect, James Henderson. Whilst the perspectives of the plan are somewhat imaginative, it shows a huge concourse and public area between Union Street and Guild Street, and extending to the west of where Bridge Street now is. Crown Terrace is clearly visible on the centre right of the picture, and the various mills and factories which at that time were located close to the centre of Aberdeen, are also evident.

The Aberdeen Railway intended to build a passenger station at Market Street, Aberdeen, on the site of the New Market, but that proposal was not carried out. Instead, in 1850, authority was obtained to alter the site to Guild Street, reducing the cost of construction works. The company was under-financed and there were many delays in building the railway due to the large number of major viaducts, rock cuttings, embankments and bridges needed. Another hazard was the lawlessness of the railway navvies, mainly Highlanders and Irish, particularly on pay days which were invariably followed by general drunkenness and the occasional riot! A major disaster in 1846 saw the collapse of several brick arches under construction at Aberdeen Ferryhill, which killed seven men and seriously injured a further four.

As a result of the many delays, it was Saturday 30th March 1850, a fortnight after the first locomotive steamed into the city, before the line officially opened for business. A local newspaper reported: "Early on that morning, a luggage train went from Ferryhill Station, and at 8 o'clock, the Directors and a party of ladies made the more formal opening trip which was performed in excellent style."

In September 1853, a second railway opened to Ferryhill, with the initial section of the Deeside Railway Company, from Aberdeen to Banchory, becoming operational. It was extended to Aboyne in 1859 and Ballater in 1866.

1854 was a busy year, with the opening, at last, of a city centre terminus at Guild Street on August 2nd. Seven weeks later, the first section of the Great North of Scotland Railway, from Kittybrewster to Huntly, also opened for traffic.

OPENING OF THE ABERDEEN RAILWAY.—DEE BRIDGE AND ABERDEEN TERMINUS.

The Illustrated London News engraving showing the opening of the Aberdeen Railway and the new Dee Viaduct. Shown, on the left, is the Ferryhill engine shed and also, on the extreme right, the Guild Street station. The illustrator has used considerable imagination with the perspectives. For four years the line used a temporary terminus at Ferryhill.

Euphoria here, however, was marred by a major catastrophe three days later, when a train arriving from the north, collided at Kittybrewster with the stock of a train about to depart, resulting in several injuries and one death. In part, this line occupied the bed of the old Aberdeenshire Canal, which sold out to the railway company.

By 1856, the Great North had extended their line to Keith, 53 miles from Aberdeen, where it was linked up, two years later, with the Inverness and Aberdeen Junction Railway, completing a connection to the Highland capital. At the Aberdeen end, passenger services were extended to a new station at Waterloo Quay. The only connection between the two railways using Aberdeen was by rails along the quayside, which were suitable only for goods wagons. Passengers changing trains either had to walk or use a horse-drawn omnibus, and connections were not guaranteed, a subject of some notoriety at the time.

During the 1850s and 1860s, the railway network extended to serve most of the North-East of Scotland. Many lines, including the Deeside Railway, were consolidated as part of the Great North of Scotland Railway. There followed much wrangling and argument over a number of rival routes to connect the two companies serving Aberdeen, including the so-called "Circumbendibus Railway". This was to run from Kittybrewster, joining with the Aberdeen Railway's successor, the Scottish North Eastern Railway, near Ferryhill. It was to cut through the city's more prestigious residential areas, such as Rosemount and Queens Cross, causing much consternation among residents.

Parliamentary powers were however obtained in 1864 for the construction of a railway from Kittybrewster through the valley of the Denburn, to a new station at Aberdeen. This opened on 4th November 1867 and was managed by a joint committee of the Great North of Scotland Railway and Caledonian Railway companies, the latter having absorbed the Scottish North Eastern Railway in 1866. In later years, the North British Railway Company, based in Edinburgh, also exercised running powers over the Caledonian line to Aberdeen, and the Joint Station thus became the terminus of three independent railway companies, with locomotives of a fourth, the Highland Railway, making appearances from 1908 onwards.

That station served its purpose for many years, but in course of time became inadequate for the increasing volume of traffic it had to deal with, including Great North of Scotland Railway suburban services to Dyce and Culter, introduced in 1887 and 1894 respectively.

A new station, much expanded from its predecessor was completed in 1915. With thirteen platforms, and adequate office, passenger circulation and siding accommodation, it was regarded as one of the most prestigious stations in Scotland. At the same time, facilities for goods and fish traffic were upgraded.

During the course of a year, the station witnessed many animated scenes, particularly during the summer season, when it was used by a large number of holidaymakers, the busiest days of the year being Aberdeen Holiday Mondays

Dating back to 1896, this interesting photograph shows GNSR Class A 4-4-0, number 6 of 1887, shunting stock in the Denburn.

and latterly the Glasgow Fair Saturday. In autumn, thousands of fisher lassies from the Buchan, Moray Firth, Orkney and Shetland fishing ports made their annual journey by train to the famous East Anglian herring fishings at Lowestoft and Yarmouth.

In 1885, Aberdeen became the northern terminus of the Up Special Travelling Post Office from Euston, at a time when the Royal Mail network was being expanded to meet the requirements of the parcel post, which came into operation in April 1883. Travelling Post Office services ceased to run north of Edinburgh and Glasgow in 1988. Competition between the East and West Coast railway companies for the Royal Mail's contracts led to them becoming embroiled in the infamous "Railway Races to the North" from London to Edinburgh in 1888, and to Aberdeen in the summer of 1895. Acceleration of services led to a week of foolhardy competition. Speed restrictions and passenger comfort and safety were ignored. The race effectively terminated at Kinnaber Junction, near Montrose, where both lines converged under the control of the Caledonian Railway's signal box, thus giving that company a tactical advantage.

The East Coast railways achieved the journey time of 8 hours 40 minutes by their shorter, but slightly more difficult route. The climax however was on the night of July 22nd/23rd 1895, when the West Coast race train, by now a fairly lightweight formation, covered the 539 miles from Euston in 8 hours 32 minutes, at an average speed of well over 60 miles per hour — a time which was not beaten until the introduction of the Inter-City 125 High Speed Trains from London to Aberdeen in 1979.

The development of road traffic saw a decline in railway operations in the

1930s, with decimation of traffic on many branch lines, and the withdrawal of the suburban services in April 1937. Long distance fish traffic also came under threat in 1937, when the well-known local road haulier, Charles Alexander, obtained licences from the Traffic Commissioners to convey fish to Manchester and elsewhere in North-West England.

The London and North Eastern and the London Midland and Scottish Railway companies, which had taken over from the Scottish pre-grouping companies in 1923, themselves became part of British Railways in 1948. Despite some modernisation of locomotives and rolling stock, there was a general downward drift in business and confidence in the railways. On the routes north of Aberdeen, many services were slower and more infrequent than in the period prior to the First World War.

A major modernisation plan for British Railways was announced in January 1955, but a prolonged rail strike later that year alienated many customers. Diesel traction, and an experimental battery electric railcar for use on the Deeside line, appeared from 1958 onwards. Steam was completely eliminated from Aberdeen in 1967, although occasional special workings using preserved locomotives have visited the city since then.

Dr. Richard Beeching, who had been appointed a few years earlier as Chairman of the British Railways Board, produced his infamous Beeching Report in 1963. Over a period of years, this led to closure of all remaining branch line

Highland Railway locomotive number 2, *Ben Alder*, on the 9.08 a.m Inverness — Aberdeen, arrives at the Joint Station on the 4th August 1911, during the period of through HR and GNSR locomotive working between the two centres. (LCGB — Ken Nunn collection)

Prior to the First World War, the goods facilities were modernised at the same time as the main station was upgraded. New sidings were laid for fish traffic on the area now occupied by the bus station. In 1961, when this picture was taken, work had just started on the demolition of the gate office in preparation for the bus station. (Aberdeen Journals)

services in the north of Scotland, including the famous Deeside line. Also closed was the original main line from Kinnaber Junction to Perth by way of Forfar and Coupar Angus. All Glasgow services were diverted by way of Dundee.

Kittybrewster Depot, at one time the main workshop of the Great North of Scotland Railway, became redundant in 1967, and all locomotives and railcars were thereafter serviced at the former Caledonian Railway's Ferryhill depot which itself closed in the 1980s.

The growth of the North Sea oil industry and a more commercial outlook on the part of British Rail, as it was by now known, led to a steady improvement of passenger services, particularly from 1979, when the Inter-City 125 High Speed Trains were introduced on London services.

Modern cost-effective Super-Sprinter type diesel trains were introduced to the Aberdeen - Inverness service as from summer 1989 and on Glasgow services from May 1990. These have largely been superseded by the air-conditioned Class 158 diesel trains now providing hourly services from the city to both Edinburgh and Glasgow for much of the day.

The Railways Act, introduced by the Conservative Government in 1994, has however led to further substantial changes, with the selling off of most parts of the railway network. A private company, Railtrack plc, now owns the infrastructure and stations. Freight operations, including locomotives and rolling stock, were also sold; the principal operator, and the only one to serve Aberdeen, being the American owned English, Welsh and Scottish Railway. Passenger services have been franchised to companies bidding on a price and quality-of-service basis.

Three passenger rail franchises now serve Aberdeen: Great North Eastern Railway, owned by the Sea Containers Group, which operates the former Inter-City services to Edinburgh and London Kings Cross; Virgin CrossCountry, jointly owned by Richard Branson's Virgin Rail Group and Stagecoach Holdings plc, which operates the daily service from Aberdeen to Plymouth, with balancing trains morning and evening to and from Edinburgh; and ScotRail, which runs all the remaining services, including the surviving overnight sleeper service to London Euston. At the time of writing, ScotRail is in the process of introducing new "Turbostar" Class 170 diesel units on services from Aberdeen to the south.

The following pages provide a brief photographic history of the first 150 years of Aberdeen's railways. What will we be celebrating 150 years from now?

Preserved steam has visited Aberdeen from time to time. In summer 1992, a series of steam trains ran on certain Sundays between Aberdeen and Elgin, with one journey to Inverness. In early September 1992, "Black 5" 4-6-0, 44871, prepares to depart from Aberdeen with the empty stock en route south to its home base at Bo'ness. Only the modern buildings in the background betray that this picture does not date from the hey-day of steam. (K. Jones)

The original Guild Street Terminus of the Aberdeen Railway, opened in 1854, after the railway extended from Ferryhill. This photograph, probably taken in the mid-1860s, was originally used as a stereoscopic slide and shows the train shed on the left, covering several tracks. To the centre of the picture, and above the cast iron water tank, is the goods shed. The Deeside Railway's goods yard is on the extreme right; a train is ready for departure. The masts of sailing ships can also be seen in the background.

At around the same time, the Denburn Valley, north of Union Bridge, was still used as a bleach green and also a recreational area for Aberdeen citizens. The Denburn was culverted during the construction of the railway. (Aberdeen City Council — Arts and Recreation Dept.)

In June 1864, the Denburn Valley Railway Act was passed by Parliament, enabling work to proceed on the construction of the line from Kittybrewster to the new Joint Station at Guild Street. This photograph shows construction of the roof of the Joint Station, probably in early 1867. The photograph was taken looking from the north, the track on the left being temporary and presumably laid to assist construction work. The scaffolding moved northwards as each segment of the roof was built. The main station buildings are on the left.

There are signs of some final tidying up work being required, which would date this picture to shortly before the formal opening of the first Joint Station on 4th November 1867. A Caledonian Railway locomotive and train sits in the single long through platform. The station also boasted several through tracks and two bay platforms at each end. An early criticism was that the station acted as a form of wind tunnel, making it draughty for passengers.

A fine shot of the old Joint Station building dating from the late nineteenth century. The main booking office is in the centre, with Caledonian Railway offices to its left and Great North of Scotland Railway offices to the right, adjacent to Guild Street.

The interior of the old Joint Station was always regarded as gloomy and dirty, and in today's vernacular was not "user friendly". This illustration, dated October 1912, shows GNSR stock on the through track to the left. By this time facilities had expanded, and a footbridge can be seen leading to the relatively new suburban platforms outwith the main train shed.

There are few pictures of passenger stock at the old Waterloo Quay Terminus, which opened to passenger traffic on 1st April 1856. There is some suggestion that this picture was taken in the 1870s, and shows number 13, one of two 0-4-0 well tanks purchased by the Great North of Scotland Railway from Messrs. Beyer Peacock of Manchester in 1855 for working the line from Kittybrewster. It is coupled to one of the early, and very basic, four wheeled carriages of the company.

Typical of secondary mainline locomotives of the mid nineteenth century, this is an 0-4-2 tender engine, built by Messrs. Hawthorn of Leith, in the 1850s. Several were bought by the Deeside Railway, but one source suggests that this is an identical engine acquired second-hand from the Banff, Portsoy and Strathisla Railway, which became number 7 in the Deeside line's fleet. The sparse accommodation for the crew can be seen. It is seen here standing at the approaches to Guild Street Station, with the paper mill, which remained in use until the 1960s, in the background.

The fascinating view looking north from Union Street in 1884. The track layout was subsequently extended at this point, as can be seen from the lower illustration. Even more interesting to an Aberdonian is the background, showing the bandstand in Union Terrace Gardens, and the various old buildings which existed prior to the construction of Rosemount Viaduct a few years later. (Aberdeen City Council — Arts and Recreation Dept.)

In contrast, the same view in 1912, showing a much expanded layout and, in the background, the platforms of Schoolhill Station. Also visible are St. Mark's Church, His Majesty's Theatre and Rosemount Viaduct itself. Today the Denburn dual-carriageway road dominates this view, with the railway reduced to a single track and a siding.

The original bridge, constructed by the Aberdeen Railway over the Dee, included wooden beams on stone foundations. From the 1880s onwards, the Caledonian Railway was undertaking a major programme of bridge improvements to accommodate heavier trains. In these pictures, probably dating from the 1890s, work is in progress on upgrading the viaduct, and on the south side of the river.

In the upper photograph, Duthie Park, presented to the city and opened in 1883, can be seen on the right. In the lower photograph, taken on the south side of the bridge, a private owner coal wagon, belonging to the local firm of Ellis and McHardy, is visible behind the steam crane. (Dr Jon Tyler collection)

Having acquired an existing hotel, the GNSR completely renovated the property at the corner of Bridge Street and Union Street. The Palace Hotel was re-opened by the GNSR in August 1891, but was subsequently extended on several occasions. It passed into LNER hands in 1923, and remained as Aberdeen's most prestigious hotel until October 1941, when it was destroyed by fire, regrettably with a number of fatalities. One feature was a direct footbridge connection to the station which can be seen in the upper photograph, just above the bridge parapets.

The upper picture, which dates from about 1903, also shows an early Aberdeen Corporation electric tramcar, heading towards Castle Street from Queens Cross.

The lower picture shows the hotel, photographed from Union Street on a wet day in the late 1930s. Also in the picture is Aberdeen's first set of traffic lights and tramcar number 1, the first of eighteen purchased second-hand from Nottingham, and which entered service in December 1936. (Aberdeen Journals)

This is the breakfast trolley used at Aberdeen on the occasion of Royal journeys to Balmoral. It was constructed in 1896 and used until 1914 for the exclusive purpose of conveying breakfast from the Palace Hotel to Aberdeen Station for members of the Royal Family, passing through on their way to Balmoral. It is now on display in the Glasgow Museum of Transport.

The interior of the Palace Hotel was lavishly furnished and generally ahead of its time as far as facilities were concerned, with electric lighting, mechanical ventilation and hydraulic lifts. Its wine cellar and cuisine was highly regarded, making the dining room, shown here, popular not only with hotel guests, but also with the Aberdonian business community. From a 1915 postcard.

ABERDEEN.

THE PALACE HOTEL

(WITHIN THE STATION),

Owned by the Great North of Scotland Railway Company.

Equipped with every modern accommodation for comfort. Electrically lighted throughout. Mechanically ventilated. Hydraulic Lifts.

EXCELLENT CUISINE.   MODERATE CHARGES.

PERSONALLY PATRONISED BY

Their Royal Highnesses the Prince of Wales, and the Duke and Duchess of Connaught, the Duke and Duchess of York, and Prince Adolphus of Teck, Princess Christian and Princess Victoria, Prince and Princess Henry of Battenberg and Prince Louis of Battenberg, Grand Duke and Grand Duchess Serge and Grand Duke Paul of Russia, and many distinguished Visitors.

COVERED WAY FROM STATION PLATFORM.

Luggage removed to and from Hotel free of charge.

Miss McKILLIAM, Manager.

Excerpt from a Paper by Captain George S. MacIlwaine, R.N., read at the Royal United Service Institution. Admiral Sir Nowell Salmon, V.C., K.C.B., in the Chair.

Unfortunately I live in hotels a great deal, and practically in all the hotels that I have seen you find Tobin's pipes to this present day. With regard to my condemnation of the Ventilation of hotels and buildings generally, I may say I except one house, that is, the hotel in Aberdeen called the Palace Hotel. That is the only house at which I ever stopped where there has been anything like a good system of Ventilation. They have an underground place in which they scrub, clean, and warm the air, and force it into the house through apertures in the walls by Blackman's fans. *Anything more delicious than the air which comes into the house you can scarcely imagine* * * * It is very pleasant to sleep in the house. You do not have to open your windows. There is a little trap over the door, and you get this delicious clean warm air into your room at once.

Today, mention of Royalty in advertising is frowned upon. The wording on this leaflet illustrates the prestige the company attached to the hotel, its accommodation and its Royal patronage.

From 1894, the GNSR was run from headquarters at 80 Guild Street, seen dominating this picture. Next to the offices sits the Station Hotel acquired by the GNSR in 1910, and which survived through LNER days to become part of the British Transport Hotels chain, until sold, along with the former railway offices, in 1983. It is now part of the Cairn Hotel Group.

This picture shows the GNSR Boardroom which still survives as meetings accommodation, having been incorporated within the hotel itself. It was characterised by an extremely ornate fireplace and polished wooden panelling.

A commercial postcard taken, probably in 1904, from outside the Station Hotel, showing, to the right of the electric tramcar on the Torry route, the offices of the Caledonian Railway and the roof of the original Guild Street station building, which at that time still formed part of the goods depot. The Criterion Bar and the Tivoli Theatre still survive today, but a high rise office block now dominates the street scene to the right.

With the introduction of suburban services by the GNSR to Dyce in 1887, an opportunity was taken, following the construction of Rosemount Viaduct, to build a station at Schoolhill, which opened in September 1893. This photograph, dated 1896, shows a train double-headed by 0-4-4 tank engine number 85, built for the suburban services in 1893, and 4-4-0 number 1 of 1879.

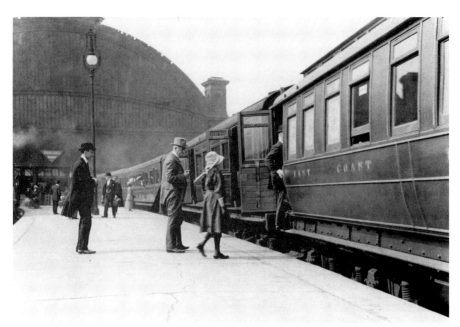

Aberdeen south end during the Edwardian era, showing the old station, and passengers joining an express for the south. The nearest carriage is part of the East Coast Joint Stock fleet, and would be a through carriage to London Kings Cross. The passengers all display evidence of prosperity, judging by their fashionable dress. (Aberdeen City Council — Arts and Recreation Dept.)

This photograph, taken by Sir Malcolm Barclay Harvey, shows the old Joint Station at its final extent, with much longer platforms and improved facilities. To reduce draughts a screen has been built to just above carriage roof level. On the left are Caledonian Railway trains; on the right, the Great North's 2.20 p.m. Deeside Express prepares to leave behind locomotive number 93 of 1895.

The old Joint Station soon proved to be inadequate for the expanding traffic of the late nineteenth century. Despite promises by the railway companies involved, it was 1908 before tangible progress was seen with new platforms and a new suburban booking office opened in 1909. Although the suburban services closed in 1937, the premises survived as a store for railway purposes until being renovated for commercial purposes. Externally, it retains its original appearance, although now known as Tiffany Hairdressing.

The suburban station platforms and extended accommodation at the north end of the station were already in place by August 1913, when this photograph was taken. The layout of platform tracks and, on the left, siding accommodation on the site of Hadden's Textile Mills, was largely in final form. The North Signal Box and the footbridge to the Palace Hotel are visible in the foreground, whilst the suburban booking office can be seen to the centre right of the photograph.

Demolition is about to begin at the south end of the old Joint Station on 20th August 1913. Work was undertaken using an electrically propelled wooden trolley surmounted by two cranes, as can clearly be seen here. There was minimum disruption to train services.

Demolition of the station roof proceeds in this picture. Various workmen pose for the photographer on 22nd October 1913. Health and Safety requirements were unsophisticated in those days.

By late October 1913, the roof is reduced to a basic framework. In this atmospheric photograph, a horse-drawn cab and, what would appear to be a horse-drawn paraffin tanker, turn from Guild Street into Bridge Street. (Aberdeen Journals)

Possibly taken about 1920, a view of the new Joint Station contrasts with the picture of the old station from a similar angle on page 14. Traffic seems sparse by today's standards. Most of the cartage work for both the Caledonian and Great North of Scotland Railways was undertaken by Messrs. Wordie and Company.

A view south from Aberdeen Station showing the complex track work and signalling which existed following the reconstruction. Denburn South Junction Signal Box can be seen in the picture. It was replaced in 1947 by a modern brick structure called Aberdeen South. This in its turn was succeeded in the early 1980s with the introduction of electronic colour light signalling equipment and by a new signalling centre.

Erected as part of the station expansion scheme, Aberdeen Centre Signal Box was opened in October 1914, on a very restricted location on platform 6. These interior and exterior pictures date from 1981, shortly before closure, and feature the duty signalman, David Tewnion. The lever frame was of Caledonian pattern with sixty levers. (Aberdeen Journals)

Whilst the Caledonian and Great North shared ownership of railway facilities in Aberdeen, the Edinburgh-based North British Railway exercised running powers over CR tracks from Kinnaber Junction, near Montrose, to Aberdeen as from 1883. In this photograph, dating from the early 1920s, North British Atlantic type 4-4-2 locomotive number 87 *Bon Accord* waits to leave with an express for Edinburgh, whilst on the right, Caledonian Class 60 4-6-0 number 64 waits with a Glasgow service.

A fine view of an ex-Caledonian Railway Dunalastair Class locomotive, number 14450, built in 1913, waiting in the Clayhills Sidings adjacent to the station with the stock of an express, including a Pullman car. This probably dates from about 1930. (Aberdeen City Council — Arts and Recreation Dept.)

With improvements of train services in 1936, the Aberdeen portion of the "Flying Scotsman" service from London was accelerated by 57 minutes. The event was sufficiently significant for Aberdeen Town Council to turn out. In this photo, Baillie Munro is shaking hands with the engine driver. The locomotive, A3 Pacific 2563, was named *William Whitelaw*, after the LNER Chairman at the time.

A more sombre occasion occurred the following April, with the withdrawal of suburban services to Dyce and Culter, after years of traffic loss. Here, in the period leading up to closure, one of the ex-GNSR 0-4-4 tank engines heads a motley selection of rolling stock towards Dyce — no match for competing road services.

An express from the south arrives at Aberdeen hauled by one of the LMS Royal Scot Class locomotives. At the time, this class of engine was used on many of the principal services of the LMS railway, with Aberdeen being their northmost destination. (A.G. Murdoch collection)

Steaming south from Aberdeen through the numerous signal gantries, an LNER fish train in the mid 1920s is hauled by Scottish Director D11 Class 4-4-0 *Lord James of Douglas*.

Waterloo continued as a goods depot until the early 1970s, when it was re-laid as a pipe yard for British Steel. Even today, some traffic is handled by the branch line from Kittybrewster which serves the private siding of Messrs. Croxton and Garry. Nearly 75 years ago, in 1926, the staff of Waterloo goods depot, plus dog, pose for the photographer. (Peter Mearns collection)

The train shed at Waterloo survived until the 1960s, but this picture is believed to date from 1937. Seen here it is accommodating a variety of goods rolling stock.

The extensive sidings at Waterloo were connected throughout their existence to the Aberdeen Harbour rails. By the time this photograph was taken, the old train shed had been demolished. In the 1970s, the whole area shown in the picture was converted for use by British Steel for pipe storage. The only areas rail-connected today are the tracks to the extreme right, which are used by Messrs. Croxton and Garry's calcium carbonate traffic.

In October 1950, a former LNER K3 Class fast freight locomotive hauls a lengthy goods train northwards past Craiginches Yard. This area to the south of the River Dee was developed by the Caledonian Railway to provide improved freight marshalling facilities. (A.G. Murdoch)

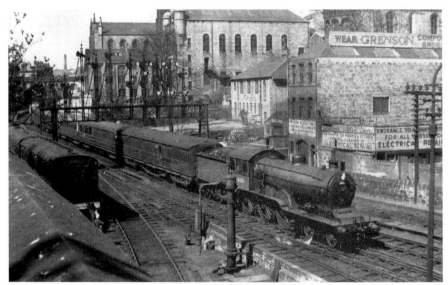

In the early 1950s, by now under British Railways' ownership, a train from the north arrives at Aberdeen behind B12 Class locomotive number 61511, which had been repainted in green livery. This was one of a batch of locomotives built by the Great Eastern Railway and transferred to North-east Scotland in the 1930s and 1940s. The track on the left foreground leads to the turntable, the site of which can still be located today. (A.G. Murdoch)

Within a few years, the B12s were replaced by more modern locomotives. Here the 4.02 p.m. Peterhead and Fraserburgh train leaves Aberdeen behind B1 4-6-0 number 61351 on 3rd July 1954, with Union Bridge in the background. At this time, signalling was still lower quadrant. (E.N.C. Haywood)

King George VI and Queen Elizabeth arrive at Aberdeen Station on 4th August, 1937 to be met by Lord Provost Watt and various Town Councillors. The carriages are from the LMS (former London and North Western Railway) Royal Train.

The particular occasion is not noted on the photograph, but here the Gordon Highlanders form a Guard of Honour for Royalty whom, on this occasion, are using the East Coast Royal Train. Note the extensive red carpeting.

At the start of the Second World War, a troop train, comprising elderly LNER rolling stock, heads south from Aberdeen to the hand waves of the friends and relatives of the soldiers on board. (Aberdeen Journals)

The post war era was one of increasing prosperity. Before the days of foreign package holidays, the Scottish Trades' holidays and, in particular, Glasgow Fair Saturday, saw the railways pressed to the limit to cater for travellers. Here, during the 1950s, large crowds wait to join southbound services at the platform barrier. (Aberdeen Journals)

Christmas at Aberdeen Station in the 1950s and 1960s was brightened up by a large Christmas tree surrounded by a working model railway. Again, this picture, from the Aberdeen Journals' archives, probably dates from the late 1950s — who can remember when cigarettes were sold for 3/10d for twenty? Switch-on of the tree was normally accompanied by a carol service, and it would appear that the plinth for the choir is under construction. (Aberdeen Journals)

The Joint Station concourse was, until 1982, dominated by the Menzies bookstall, and the large and easy to read Departures and Arrivals board. This Aberdeen Journals' photograph dates from a rail strike in February 1973, when all trains were cancelled. (Aberdeen Journals)

In February 1973, work started in demolishing the platforms at the north end of the station to make way for the office development now known as Atholl House. The Trinity Centre was also subsequently built over the same area.

By the 1970s, the ticket hall at Aberdeen Station was regarded as extremely old fashioned, with its varnished woodwork and small ticket windows. It was closed in 1978 to make way for a new travel centre, which incorporates the GNSR War Memorial. This newspaper photograph, dated January 1973, was captioned "Aberdeen Station — Scene of Last Night's Mugging"! (Aberdeen Journals)

From the outset the railways handled mail, and postal sorting carriages are believed to have run from the opening of the railway to Aberdeen. The mid-afternoon departure of the "postal" for the south on 8th August 1950 is hauled by formerly streamlined LMS Pacific 46248 *City of Leeds*. To the right, a B12 waits on a Deeside train. (A.G. Murdoch)

Postal services were withdrawn from Aberdeen in September 1988, and one of the last southbound trains waits at Aberdeen, hauled by a ScotRail Class 47 diesel locomotive. Although thirty-eight years separate these pictures, the photographer in each case was the same. (A.G. Murdoch)

A depot was established at Ferryhill at the opening of the railway to Aberdeen, and this was expanded over the years, with major reconstruction in 1908. By agreement, the Caledonian Railway permitted North British Railway locomotives to use three tracks within the building, plus certain sidings. In 1965 it still accommodates steam locomotives, although a Sulzer Type 2 (later Class 26) Diesel can be seen on the far right. (R. P. Jackson)

Britannia Class 4-6-2 70010, *Owen Glendower*, makes an impressive site on Ferryhill's turntable on 11th November 1966, having worked the early morning parcels and local passenger train from Perth. Despite dieselisation, this particular service was intermittently steam worked until May 1967. (K. Jones)

Kittybrewster was the principal depot for the Great North and, until the beginning of the century, was also the company's main workshop. These facilities were transferred to Inverurie, but the whole site was thereafter retained as a locomotive depot. This view shows the extremely cramped conditions of the workshops and probably dates from the 1890s. Great Northern Road can be seen to the left of the main roundhouse, with the freight yards on the extreme right.

A general view of Kittybrewster engine shed in the 1950s, clearly showing the roundhouse arrangement, with tracks radiating from the turntable. The tender of a B1 Class locomotive can be seen in the centre of the photograph with, in the background, a former North British Railway Class J35 goods locomotive. Kittybrewster became the area's main diesel depot in 1959.

On 31st October 1940, Kittybrewster engine shed was damaged in a bombing raid, which caused substantial injury and loss of life in Aberdeen. LNER 6843, one of the engines used to shunt at Aberdeen harbour, sustained damage in the air raid, but it appears to have been fairly superficial and the locomotive was repaired and returned to service, whilst the shed too was rebuilt.
(The late J.L. Stevenson collection)

A B12, number 61507, waits at Kittybrewster with a train from Buchan in the early 1950s, as locomotive crew make their way across the tracks, either to book on duty or to catch a tramcar home! The station closed in May 1968. (A.G. Murdoch)

GNSR Class T 4-4-0, number 105 of 1897, on a rake of coaches at Kittybrewster North, probably about 1900. The Kittybrewster North Signal Box dominates the scene, along with a curious four-armed signal.

Kittybrewster looking north from Great Northern Road bridge in British Railways days, showing part of the locomotive depot, the station building, the marshalling yards and, on the extreme right, Kittybrewster South Signal Box. The tracks immediately behind the signal box form the branch line to Waterloo.

On 7th September 1932, a Dyce to Aberdeen "subby" train, hauled by former GNSR 0-4-4T 6886 leaves Woodside Station. The train is formed of five former Great Eastern Railway carriages — note the milepost denoting $2^1/_2$ miles from Aberdeen. (E.N.C. Haywood)

Until 1975, the city boundary stopped close to the old suburban station at Persley. The building survived closure by over fifty years, until destroyed by fire. At the time of this photograph the old building was used as a private dwelling. It subsequently became a car repair workshop. On 12th August 1955, Kittybrewster based former LMS Class 2P 40648 heads into Aberdeen with a long freight. (E.N.C. Haywood)

Battery electric rail car set number SC79998/9 leaves Aberdeen on the 9.40 a.m. train to Ballater on 21st April 1958, its first day of public service. The battery electric rail car shared duties on the Ballater branch with diesel units of similar appearance until 1962, when it was withdrawn from public service. The unit however passed to the British Rail Research Department and is now preserved. Battery charging equipment was located both at Aberdeen's platform 1, and at Ballater.

The 6.30 p.m. Aberdeen to Manchester fish train storms past Girdleness on 9th June 1964, hauled by streamlined A4 Class Pacific 60004, *William Whitelaw*, which inherited its name from the locomotive shown on page 28, and former LMS Class 5 44925. The A4 Pacifics were transferred to Aberdeen in the early 1960s for working accelerated express services to Glasgow. (R. P. Jackson)

3rd September 1966 saw the last regularly scheduled steam passenger services from Aberdeen to Glasgow, although it was several months before steam was finally eliminated from the Aberdeen area. The honour of hauling the last steam worked 1.30 p.m. to Glasgow fell to Ferryhill based Class 5 44703, seen here approaching Ferryhill Junction. (R. P. Jackson)

The 1960s saw many of the branch line services from Aberdeen closed under the Beeching Plan. Northwards, only the main line from Aberdeen to Inverness survived, whilst on Sunday, 3rd September 1967, the last trains ran on the Strathmore line from Kinnaber Junction to Perth, via Forfar, the original railway route to Aberdeen. One of the short-lived Type 2 diesel locomotives built by the North British Locomotive Company of Glasgow, number D6106, leaves Aberdeen with the last southbound service via the Strathmore line, the 5.30 p.m. from Aberdeen on 3rd September 1967. (A.R. Forsyth)

As well as the main line railway systems, there were a number of industrial operations in the Aberdeen area. Foremost was the Gas Works, located in Cotton Street, which obtained its first steam locomotive *City of Aberdeen* in 1887. This is seen here entering the Gas Works, probably during the early years of the century, with some depressing tenement flats in the background. (Bon Accord Locomotive Society)

Showing the plates covering its motion, the1947 built *Mr. Therm*, built by Messrs. Andrew Barclay of Kilmarnock, the newest of four steam locomotives based at Aberdeen at the time, heads along Regent Quay in the early 1960s with coal wagons for the Gas Works. (The late N. Forrest)

In the early 1960s, the Gas Works railway obtained two diesel locomotives, a Ruston and Hornsby and a smaller Simplex. In August 1966 the Simplex heads down Church Street, with two chemical tank wagons from SAI Limited's private siding lying adjacent to the gas works, which was shunted by Gas Works' engines. (K. Jones)

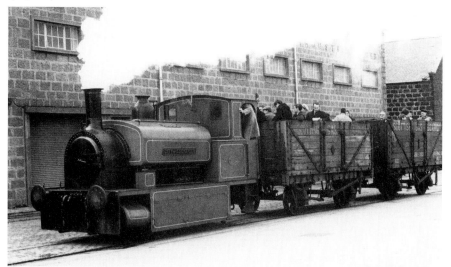

City of Aberdeen was returned to working order in 1967, after several years' disuse. It is seen working a railway enthusiast's special train in 1970. As the sharp curves on the harbour tracks restricted choice of rolling stock, passenger accommodation is not exactly luxurious! (The late N. Forrest)

The coal fired electricity works at South College Street were connected by a track along Market Street and North Esplanade opened in 1921. They were operated by battery-electric locomotives, but latterly the wagons were shunted from Guild Street yard by a British Railways' owned engine. In August 1966, the battery locomotive shunts wagons onto the coal tippler. The line was last used in early 1969. (K. Jones)

Whilst the Corporation Gas Works locomotives were able to use the Harbour tracks, the GNSR failed to reach agreement with the Harbour Commissioners until 1914, when two 0-4-2 tank locomotives were ordered from Messrs. Manning Wardle of Leeds. For a short period however, this Aveling Porter geared traction engine locomotive was borrowed, it is believed from a Speyside distillery, to shunt at the Harbour.

One of the two original locomotives ordered by the GNSR is seen at the docks in 1957. On delivery, it and its companion were found to be too heavy for the harbour tracks and two lighter engines were obtained. In later years, however, duties between the two classes became interchangeable.

Although outside the original city boundary, mention should be made of the railway at Culter Paper Mill, which connected to the Deeside line. It was originally worked by a primitive overhead-wire electric locomotive, but reverted to steam in the 1920s, when this Peckett of Bristol 0-4-0 saddle tank was acquired. It was replaced by a similar locomotive in 1954, which worked until closure of the Deeside line in 1966. (The late Peter Knight)

An unusual three feet gauge line was built by the Seaton Brick and Tile Company Limited to run from near Bridge of Don to their brick works at Black Dog, three miles to the north.

Opened in 1899 and steam worked, it provided a passenger service for workers, using some former Aberdeen Corporation horse tramcars. From 1909, passenger services were provided by a four-wheeled petrol engined rail car, built by J.B. Duff in Aberdeen.

When the brick works closed in 1924, the tramway beyond Murcar was abandoned, the remainder being acquired and operated by Murcar Golf Club. The original petrol car, which was driven from a central position, was extensively re-built in 1918 and joined in 1932 by a new forty seat four-wheeled petrol rail car built by D. Wickham and Company of Ware, Herts. The line closed in 1949.

The only known photograph of the Duff built rail car is shown above, whilst the body of the Wickham unit, as used as a store by the Golf Club into the 1960s, is also illustrated. (Aberdeen Transport Society collection)

Following the early accident at Kittybrewster, Aberdeen managed to avoid major railway disasters, but was not entirely incident free. This picture, dating from the 1930s, shows the aftermath of a derailment to a freight train south of Cove Bay. (Aberdeen Journals)

In the mid-1960s, this was the spectacular outcome of a shunting operation at Waterloo, with a van being impaled on a 350 horse power diesel shunting locomotive. The locomotive was not badly damaged and was soon repaired and back in service. (Aberdeen Journals)

Nowadays, the majority of accidents are dealt with by road crane. On 14th September 1999, the 1818 Aberdeen to Inverness service hit a mechanical digger, which had been maliciously allowed to roll on to the line from road works near the site of the former Persley Station. A major operation saw the front carriage of the Class 156 Diesel Unit being lifted on to a lorry on the Auchmill Road dual carriageway. (Aberdeen Journals)

Mention was made earlier of suburban services. In 1984, the former Dyce Station, now within Aberdeen city boundaries, which had been closed in 1968, was reopened. In this photograph, dated June 1987, the 1432 Inverness to Aberdeen approaches platform 1, with the 1625 Aberdeen to Dyce having arrived in platform 2, both worked by Class 47 locomotives. A number of Edinburgh and Glasgow to Aberdeen services now terminate at Dyce, to provide, in peak periods, a much faster service than can be achieved by road.

Aberdeen Station, 15th January 2000, shows the concourse as modernised in the 1980s, with marble tiling and glass screens, but with TV monitors providing a poor substitute for the old arrival and departure notice board. The station roof was rebuilt as part of a £3 million upgrade programme in 1998. (K. Jones)

The Clayhills sidings now see only limited use and, on 15th January 2000, were occupied only by the stock of the overnight sleeper to London, Euston, and a Class 170 Turbostar diesel unit on crew training duties. Beyond the trains can be seen the service depot, built for High Speed Trains in the late 1970s, along with the fuelling point and, in the right background, the signalling centre commissioned in 1981. (K. Jones)

Compare this picture with the photograph of Guild Street in the 1860s. The yard is still used by English, Welsh and Scottish Railways for freight traffic, but there are current proposals for a major retail and commercial development. It is already surrounded by multi-storey office blocks, but the decaying structure of the Caledonian Railways' transit shed, built prior to the First World War, can just be seen in the left background. Class 33 diesel 33030 is in the centre of the picture, with timber and container traffic obvious. This view may be substantially changed in a few years time. (K. Jones)

A brand new Scotrail Turbostar unit, 170414, pulls out of Aberdeen with the 1217 for Edinburgh on Saturday, 15th January 2000. (K. Jones)

Acknowledgements

I would like to acknowledge the help and encouragement given by fellow members of the Great North of Scotland Railway Association, with regard to the preparation of this book, particularly Dick Jackson, the late Dr. John Emslie and George Boardman, who has been responsible for layout and typesetting. Thanks also to others who have provided assistance and encouragement, including the Caledonian Railway Association, ScotRail, the staff of the Local section of Aberdeen Library at Rosemount Viaduct, Mike Dey at Aberdeen Maritime Museum, Aberdeen Journals, and with special thanks to Mrs. Maureen Shearer for typing out the draft manuscript of this book.

Photographs are, unless otherwise stated, from the collection of the Great North of Scotland Railway Association. Apologies if any specific acknowledgement has inadvertantly been omitted.

Space does not permit the setting out of the considerable bibliography of material available on Aberdeen railways. However, for further information, it is suggested that readers contact the Great North of Scotland Railway Association at the address below.

Keith G. Jones

Layout & Design —   George Boardman

Distribution —   GNSRA
78, Louisville Avenue,
Aberdeen AB15 4TX

The Great North of Scotland Railway Association
Website: www.GNSRA.org.uk

The Association was formed in 1964 to cater for all those interested in recording the history of the former Great North of Scotland Railway and its constituent companies.

Its Aims:

1. To promote the study, acquisition and preservation of information, documents and illustrations relating to all aspects of the Company.
2. To facilitate and co-ordinate research by members into the Railway's history.
3. To foster the collaboration and dissemination of the information and materials obtained.
4. To assist other private, public and professional organisations which have interests similar to those of the Association.

Membership:

Membership is open to anybody interested in furthering the aims of the Association, and further details may be obtained from: *The Membership Secretary,*
or from the website address above.   *Craighall Cottage,*
Guildtown,
Perth PH2 6DF.